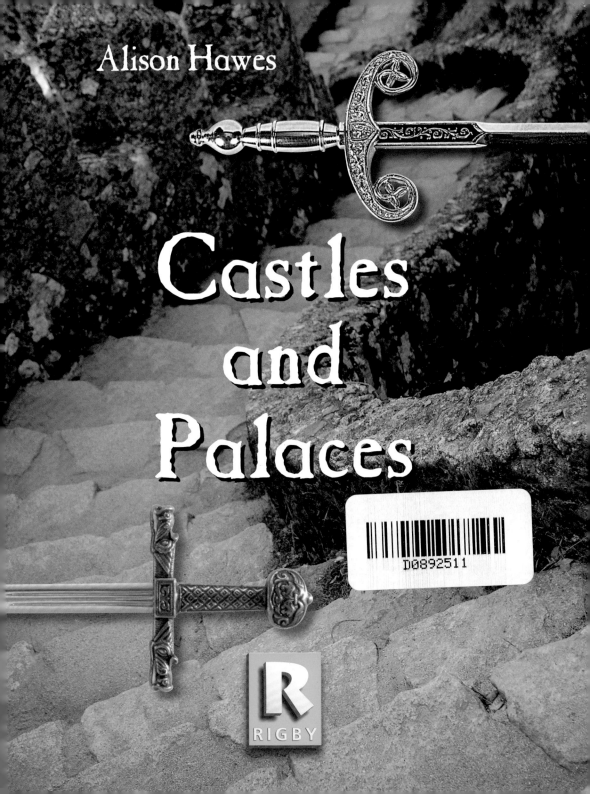

Alison Hawes

Castles and Palaces

RIGBY

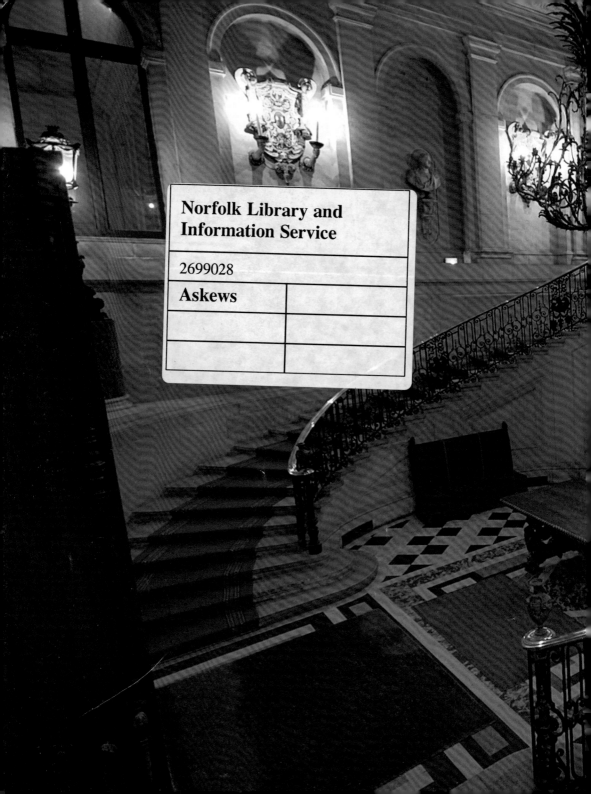

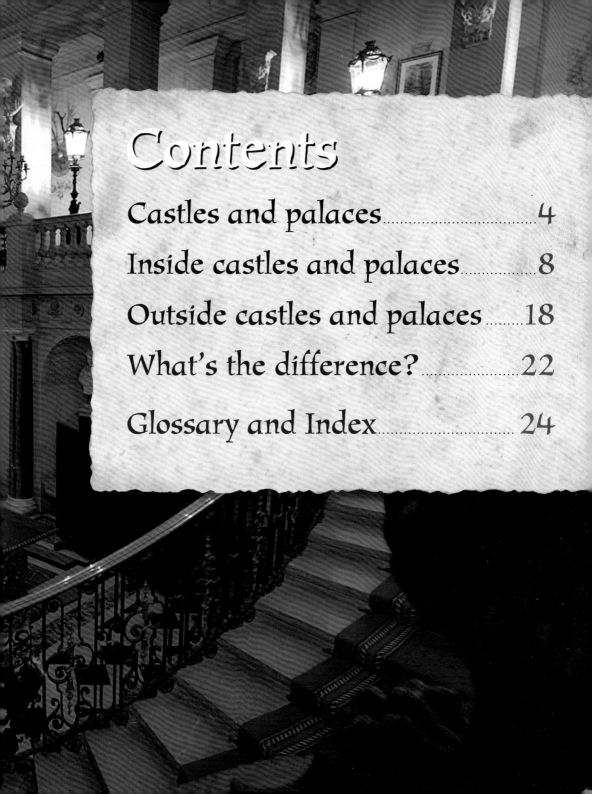

Contents

Castles and Palaces

Early castles

The first castles were built to keep important people, like kings and queens, safe. The castles had high walls and deep **moat** to keep enemies out.

The first castles were built from wood. Later, castles were built from stone. This made them stronger and safer.

This stone castle was built to keep a knight and his family safe.

Stone castles were cold and dark. So, many kings and lords moved out of them when they were not fighting. They wanted warmer homes with lots of windows and big gardens.

Lots of castles were pulled down and the stone was often used to build a new castle or palace.

The remains of a stone castle

Later castles

However, we can still see some of the old stone castles. They have been made into comfortable homes, so people can enjoy living in them. They are often called palaces.

This stone castle has been made into a comfortable home for a queen.

This castle was built by a king in Germany. He wanted to live in a castle that looked like the ones in story books.

This castle was built about 130 years ago.

The Great Hall

The most important room in an old stone castle was the Great Hall.

The Great Hall was used for:

- Dining
- Sleeping
- Meetings
- Entertaining.

The Great Hall was usually a big room with a high ceiling. It was very cold in winter because there was no glass in the windows.

Later, the halls in castles and palaces had big glass windows. Some halls had paintings and beautiful cloth hanging on the walls.

This beautiful hall is in a palace in Russia.

Dungeons

Many stone castles had dungeons. They were small, dark rooms built under the **keep** of the castle.

A dungeon was a prison where enemies were locked up. There were fleas and rats in the dungeon!

Sitting rooms

This sitting room is decorated with red cloth and gold.

Palaces had many different rooms, such as:

- Sitting rooms
- Music rooms
- Libraries
- Ballrooms
- Dining rooms.

Bedrooms

In the old stone castles, only the king or lord and his family slept in beds or had their own bedroom. Everyone else slept on straw mattresses on the floor of the Great Hall.

In the palaces, there were more bedrooms. The beds often had curtains round them.

This is a four poster bed.

Ballroom

The lords and ladies of the castle liked to dance and listen to music or stories in the Great Hall.

In palaces, special rooms were built just for dancing. These rooms were called ballrooms. Everyone wore their finest clothes to a ball.

Kitchen

Castles had huge kitchens because there were a lot of people to feed!

The food was cooked in pots or on a spit over an open fire. Bread was baked in ovens built into the castle wall.

Palace kitchens had big metal ovens and stoves to cook the food on.

Dining rooms

In the old stone castles, everyone ate their meals in the Great Hall. They sat at long wooden tables. They had knives and spoons – but no forks!

Palaces had special dining rooms. Some dining tables were very long so that lots of people could come to dinner parties.

Lighting

Castles were dark places at night because there were only candles and oil lamps to light the rooms. These did not give much light.

Palace rooms were lit with big **chandeliers** that hung from the ceiling. At first these were lit with candles. Much later, chandeliers used electricity.

Staircases

Stone castles were tall buildings, so they had lots of stairs. In the keep, the staircases were plain and made of stone or wood. In the castle towers, there were dark and narrow spiral staircases.

This staircase has a richly decorated **banister**.

Stairs in the palaces had carpets, and some were made of **marble**.

Gardens

Castle gardens were used for growing herbs, fruit and vegetables for the castle kitchen.

Many palaces had very large gardens with beautiful flowers and trees.

Lots of palace gardens also had ponds and lakes. They were made even more beautiful by adding fountains and statues.

This fountain is in the gardens at Edinburgh Castle.

Many palaces even had mazes for their guests to enjoy.

This hedge maze is in Villandry in France.

Castle animals

Some kings liked to keep wild animals in their castle grounds. They kept bears, lions and wolves. Some even kept elephants! These were the very first zoos.

Even if a castle did not keep wild animals, they might have statues of them instead.

This statue of a lion is at Arundel Castle.

What's the difference?

Old castles

Made of stone

Small windows

Lighting from candles

Dark staircases made from wood

New palaces

Made of brick

Big windows

Lighting using electricity

Wide staircases made from marble

23

Glossary

banister - the handrail and sides of a staircase

chandelier - a large hanging light with space for lots of candles or light bulbs

keep - the main tower of a castle

marble - an expensive stone used for building and statues

moat - a big wide ditch dug around a castle, often filled with water

Index